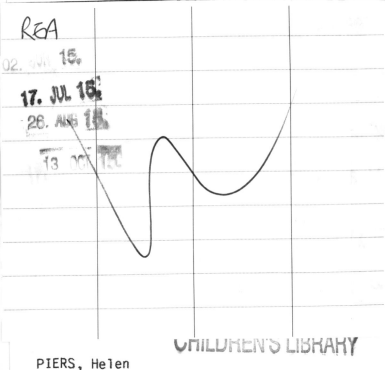

PIERS, Helen
Looking after your budgerigar

Looking after your
BUDGERIGAR

A Young Pet Owner's Guide
by Helen Piers

FRANCES LINCOLN

First published in Great Britain in 1993 by
Frances Lincoln Limited, 4 Torriano Mews
Torriano Avenue, London NW5 2RZ

The author and publishers would like to thank the children who
were photographed with their budgerigars for this book;
Cyril Laubscher (C & L Nature World) for the photograph of nestlings on page 29;
Fulham Pet Centre, London, and Caroline Ficker BVSc, MRCVS, of the
Ark Veterinary Clinics, London, for their help with the photographs
on pages 12 and 26 respectively.
Special thanks are due to Nigel Norris BVSc, MRCVS for his professional advice.

British Library Cataloguing in Publication Data
available on request

ISBN 0-7112-0769-0 hardback
ISBN 0-7112-0770-4 paperback

Printed and bound in Hong Kong

9 8 6 7 5 4 3 2 1

Contents

Budgerigars as pets

Budgerigars — or budgies for short — are a species of small parrot. They were first brought to Europe from Australia about 150 years ago, and they have adapted so well to living in captivity and proved so easy to tame that nowadays many millions of them are kept as pets all over the world.

These cheerful, intelligent little birds are not difficult to look after, and they are inexpensive to feed. But what really makes budgies such good pets is the way they enjoy human company, and take an interest in everything that is going on around them.

A tame budgerigar becomes very attached to its owner. It will come when called and sometimes even preen its owner's hair as if he or she were another bird. Some budgerigars can also learn to talk.

Wild budgerigars are found in the semi-desert lands of central Australia. They are nomadic birds, which live in large flocks. Always on the move in search of water to drink and seeding grasses on which to feed, a flock of budgerigars will often fly many miles in one day. In the summer when it becomes too hot for them and food is particularly scarce, they migrate to the south of the continent, where it is cooler.

Budgerigars never build nests and they do not return each year to the same breeding places to rear their young, as many other birds do. Wherever they happen to be, they find sheltered and convenient places, like the hollows of trees or cavities in rocks, in which to lay their eggs.

Wild budgerigars are light green, with yellow head, shoulders and wings. But pet budgerigars are bred in different shades of green, blue, mauve, yellow and white. *Pied* budgerigars have bands or patches of a second colour.

There are also *crested* budgerigars.

Is a budgerigar the right pet?

A budgerigar kept on its own needs a lot of human company, or it will be lonely. If it has to be left all by itself for several hours at a time, it is a good idea to leave the radio on, especially if it is tuned to a talks programme.

There are some things you should think about before you decide to buy a budgerigar.

Will you keep one bird or a pair?

It is natural for budgerigars to live in flocks, as they do in the wild, so if one is kept on its own it is likely to be very lonely. It will usually adopt its owner as a companion to take the place of other birds, but only if he or she can spend a lot of time with it, talking to it and having it out to play. If left alone too much, a budgerigar pines and may become ill.

If you will not have time to give your budgie the attention a single bird needs, or if it will be left alone all day when the whole family is out, it would be kinder to keep a pair. It is often believed that budgerigars kept in pairs never become tame because they have each other and do not need human company so much. But this does not have to be the case. If you have the time and patience, it is possible to keep two birds separately until they are tame, and only then put them together in the same cage (see page 16).

Will your parents or someone else in the family help you?

There will be times when you are too busy to look after and entertain your budgie, so it is important that someone else in the family is ready to help out. You will also need to plan for the holidays. Have you a friend who will look after your budgie if you go away?

Will your budgerigar get enough exercise?

Pet budgerigars do not have to fly for miles in search of food, because their food is brought to them. Even so, they need to exercise their wings, and are not really happy or healthy unless they are let out of their cage for at least an hour every day and allowed to fly freely around the room.

Have you a cat or a dog?

Keeping a budgie in the same house as a cat is very difficult. It is a cat's natural instinct to hunt birds, and a budgerigar flying around the room is easy prey. But an obedient dog will sometimes accept a bird as part of the family, and not harm it.

Budgerigars are active, intelligent birds, and easily get bored, so it is important to provide them with toys. This budgerigar has learned to climb the ladder and ring the bell at the top.

If you have more than one budgie, they may never be as tame as a single bird, but it can be very interesting watching how they behave together. They will usually preen (groom) each other and sometimes you will see one bowing its head for the other one to scratch.

Things you will need

Checklist

- cage
- sheets of sandpaper
- gravel
- feeding dishes
- water fountain or bottle
- perches
- perch brush
- food:
  seed mixture
  green vegetables
- millet spray
- cuttlefish bone
- mineral block
- grit
- clips for fixing cuttle-fish bone and millet spray to cage bars
- vitamin drops
- mite spray
- toys

A cage

Sheets of sandpaper and gravel for the floor of the cage (see NEVER box)

The cage will come supplied with perches made of dowelling or hard plastic. However, you should put in some natural branches as well – these are uneven, so the bird is less likely to get cramp or sores on its toes through always gripping with its feet in the same position (see NEVER box).

Transparent feeding dishes are best. The budgie can see the seed inside and find it more easily. You will need two small dishes for seeds and grit, and a larger one for greenstuff and fruit.

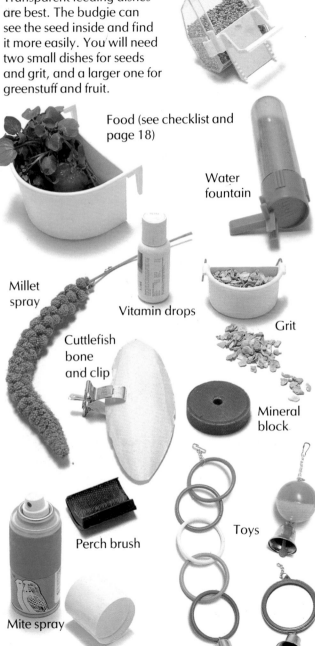

Food (see checklist and page 18)

Water fountain

Millet spray

Vitamin drops

Cuttlefish bone and clip

Grit

Mineral block

Perch brush

Toys

Mite spray

Grit should be flint or granite grit, or sea sand, mixed with oyster grit (but not white sand, sold for canaries).

A budgie easily gets bored if it has the same toys all the time, so collect quite a few and put them in the cage in rotation. A mirror helps a single bird feel less lonely. Watching its own reflection, it probably thinks there is another bird in the cage.

9

The cage

Choose the biggest cage you can afford and have room for. The ideal size for two budgerigars is about 91 × 45 cm × 45 cm high, and about two-thirds that size for a single bird.

Pet shops sell bird cages, or you may find one secondhand. There are many different types of cage to choose from, and it is worthwhile looking around to find the best. The cage is going to be your budgie's home for the whole of its life, so it is important to select one in which your budgie will be comfortable and happy.

Important points about the cage

Is it big enough?

Is it the right shape? A tall circular cage looks attractive, but does not give a bird enough space to stretch its wings.

Does the door fasten securely?

The cage should have a moulded plastic tray at the bottom which slides out to make cleaning easy.

The bars of the cage can be chromium plated or enamelled metal. Choose a cage which has at least some horizontal bars, rather than all vertical, so that your budgie can use them as a climbing frame.

Where should the cage be kept?

Budgerigars need company. Yours will be happier in a room where the family spends a lot of time. Choose a room where you can safely let your budgie out of its cage to fly about. Budgerigars need plenty of air, so the room should never be allowed to get too stuffy. A kitchen is not suitable because of cooking fumes.

Do you need a stand for the cage?

This is not essential. The cage can sit on any firm table or shelf. However, a cage on a stand takes up less space. It is also easier to move about, and is raised up high, which birds prefer.

Never

Never keep the cage in a draught, and *never* by a hot radiator or near a smoky fire.

Never keep it in the kitchen – cooking fumes are harmful and there are too many dangers for a bird flying about outside its cage (see page 22).

Never keep it directly in front of a window. It is much too cold in winter and too hot in summer.

Budgerigars can suffer stress through lack of sleep. So cover the cage with a light cloth in the evening. This should subdue the light, but not leave the bird in total darkness. (Make sure your bird will have enough air!)

Buying a budgerigar

On some young budgerigars (like the one above) the stripy head markings extend across the forehead and down to the cere. These disappear after the first moult at three months.

Most pet shops sell budgerigars, or you may be able to buy one direct from a breeder. Bird farms advertise in bird magazines.

Take your time when choosing your budgie. Watch for the ones which are more lively and active and take more interest in you when you go near the cage. A bird's colour will make no difference to its temperament or whether it will be easier to tame.

You will have to trust the breeder or pet shop assistant to know whether a young bird is a cock or a hen, because only an expert can tell at this stage.

How old should the budgerigar be?
The younger the better. By six months old a budgerigar is very difficult to tame. Six weeks is the best age, unless the bird has already been tamed by the breeder.

How can you tell how old a budgerigar is?
A six-week-old's beak may be dark or mottled, and when under three months its *cere* (the waxy swelling above the beak) is light pink, not blue or brown as in adults (see opposite).

Which sex make the best pets?

Cocks (males) and hens (females) make equally good pets. **Two cocks** or **two hens** can be kept in the same cage, or **one hen** and **one** or **two cocks**. But *two hens and one cock can never be kept together* because the hens will fight.

How do you know if a budgerigar is healthy?

Its feathers should be smooth and sleek, not spiky, and not fluffed up unless it is sleeping.

Its tail and wing feathers should not be bent or sticking out at angles.

Its breast should be well-rounded, not hollow.

Its cere should be clean, without crustiness.
Its eyes should be bright, and not runny.
It should breathe with its beak closed.

Telling a cock from a hen
The cere of an adult cock (above) is bright blue, and a hen's (below) is brown. (Exceptions are the *Pied* and *Lutino* budgerigar, both sexes of which have fleshy pink ceres.)

You will be given your bird in a cardboard box. Carry the box in your hands to avoid it getting jostled, and make your journey home as short as possible. If the weather is cold, wrap a scarf loosely around the box or hold it under your coat, but make sure the budgerigar gets enough air.

13

Getting the cage ready

Perches should be arranged so that there is one within easy reach of each food dish and the water fountain, and another higher in the cage. They should not be so close to the side of the cage that when the budgerigar perches on them its tail rubs against the bars.

To put your budgie into its cage, gently unfasten one end of the carrying box. Then hold the box just inside the open door of the cage, taking care not to leave a space through which the budgerigar can escape if it suddenly panics. If it does not hop out at once, you can tilt the box a little.

If possible, prepare the cage before you go out to buy your budgie (or pair of budgies, if you have decided to keep two).

First, wash the whole cage in very hot water. Do not use soap or detergent, and only use disinfectant if it is the kind sold especially for bird cages. If you use a secondhand cage, you *must* disinfect it.

Dry the cage thoroughly.

Lay a sheet of sandpaper on the cage floor, and cover it with a sprinkling of gravel. Then arrange the perches, the dishes for seed and grit, and the water fountain. The cuttlefish bone, millet spray, and mineral block should be clipped to the bars of the cage.

The first few weeks

Once your budgie is safely in its cage, it is best to leave it quiet and by itself in the room for two or three hours.

Budgerigars are brave little birds, but even so, your new budgie will find everything very unfamiliar and even frightening, and it may be homesick. So for the first week or two it is very important to make sure it is not alarmed by loud noises, or anything else that might be stressful (see NEVER box). Take care that the cage does not face the TV and is not near a harsh light, but avoid leaving your budgie in complete darkness. At night there should be some form of dim light in the room.

If you have bought two budgerigars they will be more confident. Even so, you should keep things as calm and quiet as you can.

Sometimes it takes a while for a young budgie to find the seed inside a seed dish, so it is a good idea to sprinkle a little on the cage floor until you know for sure that it is eating from the dish. Remember, budgerigars need to eat little but often.

At first, when you clean the cage or bring food to your new budgie it will probably show alarm. Reassure it by talking softly all the time, and move quietly and gently. When it no longer retreats into a corner or flutters about, and perhaps begins to show interest in what you are doing, then you will know it is feeling at home, and you can begin taming it.

Never

Especially during the first week or two:
Never shout loudly, slam doors, or have TV or radio on too loud.
Never leave windows wide open on to a street. Cars and sirens may alarm your bird.
Never make sudden movements near the cage, or approach it suddenly.
Never press your face against the bars.

Once you see your budgie pecking at its food, you will know it is beginning to feel less strange in its new home.

15

All the time and patience you spend on taming your budgie will seem well worthwhile when at last it comes to your hand in answer to its name.

Taming

To tame your budgie you will need to overcome its fear and win its trust. This may take some weeks, so be patient. Follow the method opposite and remember to be gentle and talk soothingly at the same time.

It is best if only one person tries to tame a budgerigar. If the whole family 'has a go', your bird may get confused. No one else should be in the room during taming, and the TV or radio should be switched off.

If you are keeping two birds together you should be able to win their trust by using the same method, although they will probably never become as tame as a single bird.

If you have started off with one budgie, you may feel later that it would be happier with a companion. If you decide to buy a second budgerigar, and your first budgie is already tame, it is a good idea to tame the second bird before you put them together.

You will need to keep the new bird in a separate room until it is tame, and let the two birds get to know each other gradually. First, you can put their cages in the same room. Then, after a week or so, you can let them fly about the room together. But watch carefully, and only put them in the same cage when you are sure they are going to be friends.

In this way you will have two budgies which are both tame, and yet will never be lonely.

1 To teach your budgie not to fear your hand, begin by offering it a piece of millet through the cage door. Hold the millet so the bird can reach it, but keep your hand below its head and not too close. It will probably retreat into a corner or flutter about in alarm. But leave your hand there for a few minutes.

2 Offer the millet frequently, even every two or three hours. After a few days your budgie should overcome its fear and begin to peck at it. Then move your hand closer and hold it so that the bird has to hop on to your finger to reach the millet. When it does, take care not to jerk your hand in the excitement.

3 When your budgie has lost its fear of your hand you can offer your forefinger to it as a perch (without the millet). Press the finger gently against the bird's lower breast, and encourage it by talking softly to it, and saying its name. Be patient – budgerigars are very suspicious of anything new.

4 When your budgie has begun to hop confidently on to your finger you can gently lift it out of the cage. It is important to finger-tame your budgie before you let it out to fly around the room. Catching a bird which does not come to your finger when it is time to return to its cage is not easy, and can be frightening for the bird.

Feeding 1

Budgerigars feed on the seeds of grasses, some fresh green food and a little fruit.

Seeds

Pet shops sell packeted seeds specially mixed to give budgerigars a balanced diet. Make sure the packet is labelled 'budgerigar seed' – not just 'bird seed'.

It is important that the seed is fresh. So only buy enough for two months at a time and never store it in a plastic bag – it needs air, or it will go mouldy. Seed is best stored in a cloth bag, or in a closed tin *with air holes punched in the lid*, and kept in a cool dry place.

Take care your budgie is never left without seeds to eat. Budgies only eat the kernels, leaving the husks to pile up. You may think the dish is full of seeds, when it is only full of husks.

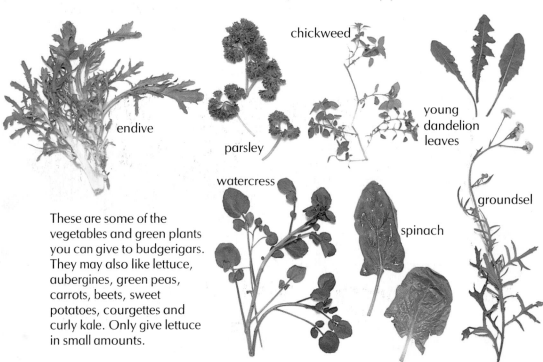

endive

chickweed

parsley

young dandelion leaves

watercress

spinach

groundsel

These are some of the vegetables and green plants you can give to budgerigars. They may also like lettuce, aubergines, green peas, carrots, beets, sweet potatoes, courgettes and curly kale. Only give lettuce in small amounts.

Green food and fruit

At first your budgie may not touch any green food or fruit. It may never have been given fresh food before. Continue to put some out just the same. In time your budgie will pluck up courage and try it, and you will find out which foods it likes best. Do not give too much fruit. A small piece every two days is enough.

Extra foods

During winter and when birds are moulting or breeding they need extra nourishment, and enjoy occasional treats of wheat germ, oats, or sunflower seeds. Once a week you can give your budgie a teaspoon of hard-boiled egg mixed with cottage cheese.

Your budgie will enjoy pecking at a millet spray as a treat. This is also very nutritious food. But millet is fattening, so only give about two inches of spray a day.

orange (or tangerine)

apples

strawberries

grapes

tomato

pear

cherries

All these fruits are good for budgerigars. (You can also give blackberries, apricot, pineapple, banana, kiwi fruit and mango.)

Remember

- Always make sure there is some food in the cage.
- Give a good variety of fresh green food and fruit.
- Wash green food (especially lettuce) and fruit well to remove traces of pesticides.
- Remove fresh food if not eaten the same day.
- Make sure grit is always available.
- **Give fresh water every day.**

Vitamin drops

To make sure your budgie is getting enough vitamins, it is very important to add vitamin drops (sold at pet shops) to its drinking water.

Cuttlefish bone and mineral block

Pecking at a cuttlefish bone gives a budgerigar valuable calcium, and a mineral block provides all the minerals it needs. Both can be clipped to the bars of the cage.

If you buy a cuttlefish bone from the pet shop it will already be prepared. But if you pick one up on the beach you will need to clean it, boil it for one hour, then leave it to soak for a week, changing the water daily.

Grit

Birds have no teeth so they have to swallow grit of some kind to help grind up the food in their gizzard (part of a bird's stomach). Some grit should always be available, either in a dish or sprinkled on the cage floor.

How much food and how often?

How much food a budgerigar needs depends on its age, how much exercise it is getting, and its own individual appetite. The important thing is to make sure there is always some food in the cage, because budgerigars need to eat little but often. Follow the plan opposite and you will know you are giving your bird enough food. Budgerigars rarely overeat unless they are very bored and lonely.

By pecking at a cuttlefish bone, a budgerigar sharpens its beak as well as getting the calcium it needs. It has a curved beak, specially shaped for taking the husks off seeds.

Feeding Plan
In the morning
Clean out seed dish and fill with seed. Give fresh drinking water.

Two or three times during the day
Remove empty husks from seed dish (you can blow them off or remove with a small spoon) and top up with fresh seed. If you are going to be out all day it is best to leave two dishes of seed as a budgerigar will often go hungry because it cannot find the uneaten seeds hidden under empty husks.

Every other day
Give a small handful of green food and a piece of fruit.

Never

Never give kitchen scraps or chocolate.
Never let the seed go mouldy.
Never give frozen, cooked or canned vegetables and fruit.
Never give fruit or vegetables straight from the fridge – all food should be at room temperature.
Never gather plants from beside a road, because of pollution.

You can give fresh food in a dish or poke it through the bars of the cage for the budgerigar to peck at.

Flying outside the cage

Once your budgie is tame you should let it fly outside its cage as much as possible – for at least an hour a day.

Is the room escape-proof?

Make sure all doors and windows are shut *completely*. Budgerigars can fly through very narrow gaps. They can also hurt themselves trying to fly through closed windows, because they cannot see the glass. So windows should be curtained or covered in some way. (For other dangers, see the REMEMBER box.)

The first flight outside the cage

The cage will have become the place where your budgie feels safe, and it may be afraid to come out and explore the room. So first lift it out on your finger. Let it perch on top of the cage to look around and decide when it feels safe enough to fly about. Eventually it will take off, fly around the room and probably settle somewhere high up. It may stay up there a long time, panting with agitation, because leaving its cage for the first time is a big adventure for a young bird. Talk to it reassuringly, but do not try to persuade it to come down.

Your budgie may be unable to find its way back to its cage, or be too frightened to make the return flight. You can help by lifting the cage up closer to it. But you may have to wait until hunger gives the budgie enough courage to return by itself.

Never try to shoo your budgie back to its cage by waving things at it. Avoid giving it food outside the cage, or it may not be so ready to fly back in. In an emergency, the best way to catch a budgerigar is to throw a duster or small piece of lightweight cloth over it, then very gently pick it up with your hands over its *closed* wings.

Will the budgerigar do any damage?

It might peck at the wallpaper or books. If it does, you can pin paper over any piece of wall close to the places where it likes to perch, and cover bookcases temporarily with a cloth. Budgerigar droppings do not stain, and when dry they can be vacuumed up.

You can make a special perching place for your budgie, using small branches and bamboo. Train an indoor plant to climb up and over them; then hang them with toys. But avoid using any poisonous plants (see REMEMBER box).

The more you play with your budgie, the more friendly it will become. You can train it to climb ropes, ring bells and roll plastic balls or marbles about – it will enjoy rolling them off the table for you to pick up.

Cleaning

It is important to keep the cage very clean if your budgie is to stay healthy and be free from parasites.

Once a day
Wash seed dishes in hot water, and dry well before refilling. Remove husks, droppings and uneaten food from floor tray. Wipe perches and bars of cage with damp (not wet) cloth.

Once a week
Empty floor tray and wash in very hot water. *Dry thoroughly.* Put in fresh sandpaper or gravel. Scrub perches, and if worn smooth, rub over with sandpaper to roughen them. Wash toys and ladders.

Once a month
Scrub out whole cage in very hot water. *Rinse and dry well.* **Never** use soap or detergent, which are harmful to birds. Spray with mite spray (from pet shop).

Cleaning is best done during the budgerigar's free flight time. The cage (*and the perches*) must be thoroughly dry before the bird returns to it.

Preening and bathing

A budgerigar keeps its feathers clean and in good condition by preening, and it can do this better if its feathers are *slightly* damp.

Once every two days, you can give your budgie a saucer of lukewarm water – no more than 2 cm deep – to splash in. Alternatively, you can spray your bird *lightly*. Use a plant sprayer, but make sure it produces a fine spray, not a jet of water. Only give bath water or spray before midday, so your bird's feathers will be dry by evening. Keep it out of draughts while it is still damp.

Do not give your bird bath water or spray it in very cold weather.

You can buy a bird bath to fix across the open cage door. A sprig of parsley in the water encourages the bird to use it.

A budgerigar preens itself by pulling each tail and wing feather in turn through its beak to remove dust and dirt, and pecks and smooths down its soft feathers.

Health and illness

Remember

You will help your budgies stay healthy if you:

- Give them a good variety of fresh green food.
- Give extra vitamins, calcium and minerals (see page 20).
- Keep them out of draughts, and do not let them get too hot or too cold.
- Make sure they get sunshine, but *not* hot midday sun, especially through glass.
- Never let them get lonely or bored.
- Keep the cage clean.

Budgerigars rarely get ill, but when they do, they quickly lose condition, so never put off getting help from a veterinary surgeon.

How do you know if a budgerigar is ill?
Apart from the symptoms given on the next page, a sick budgerigar will take no interest in what is going on, and its eyes will be dull. It will sit low on its perch, huddled up, with feathers fluffed out. It may be off its food, and be more thirsty than usual.

What do you do if your budgerigar is ill?
There is some advice on the next page. But it is hard to be sure what is the matter with a bird, so it is best to phone the vet's surgery and describe your bird's symptoms. The vet will advise you what to do.

Meanwhile make sure your budgie is in a quiet, warm place, and has water to drink.

Often a budgerigar's beak and claws grow too long. If this happens your vet will clip them painlessly. Do not try to do this yourself.

If your bird has an accident and breaks a leg or a wing it is better to take it to the vet, rather than try to treat it yourself.

Symptoms	Possible cause and what to do
Loss of feathers	All birds *moult* – shed their old feathers and grow new ones – from time to time. Baby budgerigars moult at three months, and adults some time during summer or autumn. But if your bird has bald patches **take it to the vet**. It could have *red mites* or some other parasite. If it continually plucks out feathers, then it may be lonely, or have an *allergy*.
A whitish grey crust appears on the beak and gradually spreads to the cere, around the eyes and on the feet	This is *scaly face*, and is caused by a tiny parasite. The bird should be isolated from other birds, because scaly face is catching. The vet will give you a lotion with which to treat it.
Breathing with beak open, discharge from nostrils, rattling noises in throat	The budgerigar has a cold, or maybe a more serious respiratory infection. **Take it to the vet at once**, but take care to cover the cage or carrying box so it does not get cold.
The droppings are runny and discoloured	The bird has *diarrhoea*. Maybe it has eaten something which did not agree with it, but diarrhoea can be a sign of a more serious illness, so keep the bird warm, remove green food, and **telephone your vet for advice**.
The bird is straining as if it is having trouble passing its droppings	It may be *constipated*. Give extra green food. If no better in 24 hours **take it to the vet**. But if it is a *hen bird* and seems in pain, she may be having difficulty laying an egg. This could be serious – even fatal – **so take her to the vet at once**. (Hens lay eggs even if they have no mate.)

Breeding budgerigars

There is only space in this book to give a little information on breeding, but if you are seriously interested in raising young, there are other books which will tell you all you need to know (see page 31).

Best age to breed
Hen budgerigars can lay eggs at three to four months but it is best to wait until they are fully grown at 10 to 11 months before letting them mate and rear a brood of chicks.

Mating
Pet budgerigars can breed all the year round. When in mating condition, the cock bird's cere becomes very bright blue and the hen's dark brown. You know budgerigars are ready to mate when the cock begins to court the hen by singing to her while puffing up his head and throat feathers, and feeds her regurgitated food. They preen each other and rub beaks.

Budgerigars will not breed unless they have a nesting box. Pet shops sell them, or you can make your own. The box should be about 15 × 24 cm and 14 cm high. It can have a hinged lid so that you can check on the young birds from time to time, or sliding glass and wood panels, as shown.

The shallow hollow in the base is to prevent the eggs from rolling about. If the birds roll any of the eggs out of the nesting box it means they are not fertilized and no babies can hatch out of them.

Egg-laying and incubation
After mating, the cock must be left with the hen, for her eggs will not mature inside her unless she can hear him singing. Also he will feed her while she is sitting on the eggs, and help to rear the brood.

Within two weeks of mating, the hen will lay her eggs. At this time the cage should be kept in a warm room and the air never allowed to get too dry.

Budgerigar hens usually lay five or six eggs. They lay them one at a time, on every other day. Once she has begun to lay her eggs, a hen will sit on them to keep them warm and incubate them, hardly ever leaving the nesting box. Until the baby birds hatch out she relies on the cock to bring her food.

At 18 days the baby birds begin to hatch out – one every other day, in the order in which the eggs were laid.

The baby budgerigars

Baby budgies are born helpless and blind, and totally dependent on the parents to keep them warm under their feathers and feed them. But they develop quickly, and in four weeks they can already fly. At this age they begin to leave the nesting box, but they should stay with their parents for another two weeks.

Budgerigars usually pair for life unless, of course, they are separated for some reason. These two are *pied* budgerigars.

In the wild, baby budgerigars have to be ready to fly with the flock when it migrates, so budgerigar chicks develop quickly. At six days their eyes open, and at seven days their feathers begin to grow. After 10 days they are covered with down. At four weeks their wing and tail feathers are nearly fully grown.

Teaching your budgerigar to talk

If you want your budgie to talk you must start teaching it when it is very young, and be patient, because it may take several months to learn. Teaching sessions should last only 10 minutes, but they can be repeated as often as every two hours.

Begin by teaching your budgie its name. Once it has learned to say this clearly, start to teach it other words – one at a time – and then short phrases. A good talker may manage quite long sentences after a while.

When teaching your budgie to talk, hold it on your finger close to your face and repeat the word you want it to learn many times over. Do not shout, but speak loudly and distinctly, and always say the word in the same way. As with taming, only one person should try to teach a budgerigar to talk. There should be nobody else in the room, and no distraction from a TV or radio.

Don't give up easily, but do not be disappointed if your bird does not respond – some budgies can never be trained to talk.

Understanding your budgerigar

How does a budgerigar show it is happy?
A happy budgerigar will eat well, sing, and generally be busy, either preening its feathers or playing with its toys.

How does a budgerigar show it is afraid?
It may retreat into a corner of the cage, pull itself up tall and thin, or flutter around the cage. When its fright is over and it feels safe again it often fluffs up its feathers and gives itself a good shake before it settles down.

How does it show it is pleased to see you?
It will hop towards you, and bob its head up and down. If it is on your shoulder it may preen your hair.

How does it behave when it wants to be left alone to sleep?
When it is ready to sleep, a budgerigar retires to its favourite perch, fluffs up its feathers and perches on one leg, with the other drawn up under it. Often it buries its head in its feathers.

Your budgie may live to be 10 or even up to 18 years old, and all through its life it will depend on you for everything it needs – it cannot look after itself and have the companionship of other birds as it would in the wild. So take good care of it, play with it, and make its life as interesting as possible. In return, it will give you a lot of fun and enjoyment.

Further reading

Care for your Budgerigar
RSPCA Official Pet Guide
Tina Hearne
Collins, 1990

The New Parakeet Handbook
I. Birmelin / A. Wolter
Barron's, 1986
(very helpful on breeding)

Parakeets
C. Feyerabend
TFH Publications, 1984

Index